# Happy 1st Birthday

_____

Date _____

# Guest

_____

_____

## Birthday Wish

_____
_____
_____

## Special Message to the Parents

_____
_____
_____

# Guest

## Birthday Wish

## Special Message to the Parents

# Guest

_____

_____

## Birthday Wish

_____

_____

_____

## Special Message to the Parents

_____

_____

_____

# Guest

## Birthday Wish

## Special Message to the Parents

# Guest

## Birthday Wish

## Special Message to the Parents

# Guest

_____

_____

## Birthday Wish

_____

_____

_____

## Special Message to the Parents

_____

_____

_____

# Guest

_____

_____

## Birthday Wish

_____

_____

_____

## Special Message to the Parents

_____

_____

_____

# Guest

## Birthday Wish

## Special Message to the Parents

# Guest

## Birthday Wish

## Special Message to the Parents

# Guest

## Birthday Wish

## Special Message to the Parents

# Guest

_____

_____

## Birthday Wish

_____

_____

_____

## Special Message to the Parents

_____

_____

_____

# Guest

_____

_____

## Birthday Wish

_____

_____

_____

## Special Message to the Parents

_____

_____

_____

 # Guest

_____

_____

## Birthday Wish

_____

_____

_____

## Special Message to the Parents

_____

_____

_____

# Guest

_____

_____

## Birthday Wish

_____

_____

_____

## Special Message to the Parents

_____

_____

_____

 # Guest

_____

_____

## Birthday Wish

_____

_____

_____

## Special Message to the Parents

_____

_____

_____

# Guest

## Birthday Wish

## Special Message to the Parents

# Guest

_____

_____

## Birthday Wish

_____
_____
_____

## Special Message to the Parents

_____
_____
_____

## Guest

_____

_____

### Birthday Wish

_____

_____

_____

### Special Message to the Parents

_____

_____

_____

# Guest

_____

_____

## Birthday Wish

_____

_____

_____

## Special Message to the Parents

_____

_____

_____

# Guest

_____

## Birthday Wish

_____
_____
_____

## Special Message to the Parents

_____
_____
_____

# Guest

_____

_____

## Birthday Wish

_____

_____

_____

## Special Message to the Parents

_____

_____

_____

# Guest

_____

_____

## Birthday Wish

_____

_____

_____

## Special Message to the Parents

_____

_____

_____

# Guest

_____

_____

## Birthday Wish

_____

_____

_____

## Special Message to the Parents

_____

_____

_____

# Guest

_____

_____

## Birthday Wish

_____

_____

_____

## Special Message to the Parents

_____

_____

_____

# Guest

## Birthday Wish

## Special Message to the Parents

## Guest

_____

### Birthday Wish

_____

_____

_____

### Special Message to the Parents

_____

_____

_____

## Guest

_____

_____

## Birthday Wish

_____

_____

_____

## Special Message to the Parents

_____

_____

_____

# Guest

_____

_____

## Birthday Wish

_____

_____

_____

## Special Message to the Parents

_____

_____

_____

# Guest

_____

_____

## Birthday Wish

_____

_____

_____

## Special Message to the Parents

_____

_____

_____

# Guest

_____

## Birthday Wish

_____
_____
_____

## Special Message to the Parents

_____
_____
_____

## Guest

_____

_____

### Birthday Wish

_____

_____

_____

### Special Message to the Parents

_____

_____

_____

# Guest

_____

_____

## Birthday Wish

_____

_____

_____

## Special Message to the Parents

_____

_____

_____

# Guest

_____

_____

## Birthday Wish

_____

_____

_____

## Special Message to the Parents

_____

_____

_____

# Guest

_____

_____

## Birthday Wish

_____

_____

_____

## Special Message to the Parents

_____

_____

_____

# Guest

_____

_____

## Birthday Wish

_____
_____
_____

## Special Message to the Parents

_____
_____
_____

# Guest

_____

_____

## Birthday Wish

_____

_____

_____

## Special Message to the Parents

_____

_____

_____

 # Guest

_____

_____

## Birthday Wish

_____

_____

_____

## Special Message to the Parents

_____

_____

_____

# Guest

_____

_____

## Birthday Wish

_____

_____

_____

## Special Message to the Parents

_____

_____

_____

# Guest

_____

_____

## Birthday Wish

_____

_____

_____

## Special Message to the Parents

_____

_____

_____

# Guest

## Birthday Wish

## Special Message to the Parents

# Guest

_____

_____

## Birthday Wish

_____

_____

_____

## Special Message to the Parents

_____

_____

_____

# Guest

_____

_____

## Birthday Wish

_____

_____

_____

## Special Message to the Parents

_____

_____

_____

# Guest

_____

_____

## Birthday Wish

_____

_____

_____

## Special Message to the Parents

_____

_____

_____

 # Guest

_____

_____

## Birthday Wish

_____

_____

_____

## Special Message to the Parents

_____

_____

_____

# Guest

## Birthday Wish

## Special Message to the Parents

# Guest

## Birthday Wish

## Special Message to the Parents

# Guest

_____

_____

## Birthday Wish

_____

_____

_____

## Special Message to the Parents

_____

_____

_____

# Guest

_____

_____

## Birthday Wish

_____

_____

_____

## Special Message to the Parents

_____

_____

_____

# Guest

## Birthday Wish

## Special Message to the Parents

# Guest

## Birthday Wish

## Special Message to the Parents

# Gifts

| Date | Gift received | Given by | Thank you note sent |
|------|---------------|----------|---------------------|
|  |  |  | ☐ |
|  |  |  | ☐ |
|  |  |  | ☐ |
|  |  |  | ☐ |
|  |  |  | ☐ |
|  |  |  | ☐ |
|  |  |  | ☐ |
|  |  |  | ☐ |
|  |  |  | ☐ |
|  |  |  | ☐ |
|  |  |  | ☐ |
|  |  |  | ☐ |
|  |  |  | ☐ |
|  |  |  | ☐ |
|  |  |  | ☐ |
|  |  |  | ☐ |
|  |  |  | ☐ |
|  |  |  | ☐ |
|  |  |  | ☐ |
|  |  |  | ☐ |
|  |  |  | ☐ |
|  |  |  | ☐ |
|  |  |  | ☐ |
|  |  |  | ☐ |
|  |  |  | ☐ |
|  |  |  | ☐ |

| Date | Gift received | Given by | Thank you note sent |
|------|---------------|----------|---------------------|
|  |  |  | ☐ |
|  |  |  | ☐ |
|  |  |  | ☐ |
|  |  |  | ☐ |
|  |  |  | ☐ |
|  |  |  | ☐ |
|  |  |  | ☐ |
|  |  |  | ☐ |
|  |  |  | ☐ |
|  |  |  | ☐ |
|  |  |  | ☐ |
|  |  |  | ☐ |
|  |  |  | ☐ |
|  |  |  | ☐ |
|  |  |  | ☐ |
|  |  |  | ☐ |
|  |  |  | ☐ |
|  |  |  | ☐ |
|  |  |  | ☐ |
|  |  |  | ☐ |
|  |  |  | ☐ |
|  |  |  | ☐ |
|  |  |  | ☐ |
|  |  |  | ☐ |
|  |  |  | ☐ |
|  |  |  | ☐ |
|  |  |  | ☐ |

| Date | Gift received | Given by | Thank you note sent |
|------|---------------|----------|---------------------|
|      |               |          | ☐ |
|      |               |          | ☐ |
|      |               |          | ☐ |
|      |               |          | ☐ |
|      |               |          | ☐ |
|      |               |          | ☐ |
|      |               |          | ☐ |
|      |               |          | ☐ |
|      |               |          | ☐ |
|      |               |          | ☐ |
|      |               |          | ☐ |
|      |               |          | ☐ |
|      |               |          | ☐ |
|      |               |          | ☐ |
|      |               |          | ☐ |
|      |               |          | ☐ |
|      |               |          | ☐ |
|      |               |          | ☐ |
|      |               |          | ☐ |
|      |               |          | ☐ |
|      |               |          | ☐ |
|      |               |          | ☐ |
|      |               |          | ☐ |
|      |               |          | ☐ |
|      |               |          | ☐ |
|      |               |          | ☐ |

| Date | Gift received | Given by | Thank you note sent |
|------|---------------|----------|---------------------|
|      |               |          | ☐ |
|      |               |          | ☐ |
|      |               |          | ☐ |
|      |               |          | ☐ |
|      |               |          | ☐ |
|      |               |          | ☐ |
|      |               |          | ☐ |
|      |               |          | ☐ |
|      |               |          | ☐ |
|      |               |          | ☐ |
|      |               |          | ☐ |
|      |               |          | ☐ |
|      |               |          | ☐ |
|      |               |          | ☐ |
|      |               |          | ☐ |
|      |               |          | ☐ |
|      |               |          | ☐ |
|      |               |          | ☐ |
|      |               |          | ☐ |
|      |               |          | ☐ |
|      |               |          | ☐ |
|      |               |          | ☐ |
|      |               |          | ☐ |
|      |               |          | ☐ |
|      |               |          | ☐ |

| Date | Gift received | Given by | Thank you note sent |
|---|---|---|---|
| | | | ☐ |
| | | | ☐ |
| | | | ☐ |
| | | | ☐ |
| | | | ☐ |
| | | | ☐ |
| | | | ☐ |
| | | | ☐ |
| | | | ☐ |
| | | | ☐ |
| | | | ☐ |
| | | | ☐ |
| | | | ☐ |
| | | | ☐ |
| | | | ☐ |
| | | | ☐ |
| | | | ☐ |
| | | | ☐ |
| | | | ☐ |
| | | | ☐ |
| | | | ☐ |
| | | | ☐ |
| | | | ☐ |
| | | | ☐ |
| | | | ☐ |

Made in United States
Orlando, FL
21 December 2023